Spoken Medicine

Gabrielle Journey Jones
Spoken Medicine

Acknowledgements

Some poems appear on the Creative Womyn Down Under website as videos and in print at www.creativewomyn.net/gabejourney.html

I dedicate this collection to my children

Jai Jones and Sofara Jones
The creative sparks of many hearts
The rhythms inside my rhymes
I love you both, always
(All. The. Time.)
– Mumma Gabe

Spoken Medicine
ISBN 978 1 76041 430 6
Copyright © text Gabrielle Journey Jones 2017
Cover art by Amalina Wallace

First published 2017 by
Ginninderra Press
PO Box 3461 Port Adelaide 5015 Australia
www.ginninderrapress.com.au

Contents

Freedom	9
Freedom Rap	11
Fire Belly Feminism	15
Weightless	17
Humanitarian	19
Equalities	21
Racism: Call It Out	22
Spirituality Is In	23
Mind Journey	25
Peace	26
Wise Woman	27
Creativity	29
Spoken Medicine	31
Creative Expression	33
The Problem With Poets	34
Poetry What?	35
Poetry Lab	37
A Poem Is Born	38
Birthing Magic	39
Written Word	40
Fifteen Reasons I Write	42
Ballpoint Pen	43
Artist Circles	44
Advice On What To Wear To a Poetry Reading	45
Drumming Womyn	46
Drum Flow	47
Djembe Dance	48
Drum Song Sonnet	49
The Happen'n Drum Camp New York 2008	50

National Folk Festival 2008 – Folky Rap	51
National Folk Festival 2016 – Folky 50th	52
Dear Grace Cossington Smith	53

Family   55

Jai	57
Sofara	58
Holidays	59
Babies	61
Unbreakable	62
I Used To Write	63
Ancestors	64
Sweet Sherry	65

Identity   67

Gabrielle	69
Adoption Belonging	71
Journey MC	73
Flowetry	74
Simply Me	75
Forty-four	76

Gratitude

Thank you to my family and friends who have encouraged me to write and share my poetry. Much love and respect to my parents, Patricia and Alan Jones who have graciously led the cheer squad for my forty-four years of creative expression.

Deep appreciation for the passionate gatherings of poets that I've been lucky enough to meet and enjoy the 'welcoming balm of spoken word community' ('Spoken Medicine').

Big love and gratitude for our creative adventures that have inspired my writing: Julia Jacobs, Corinne Roberts and Mystral Ford (Tranceportation), Ca$h Flo (Revoluvtion), Rebecca Gould and Kerri Ellis (Unpublished Poetry Lab), Mignon Lee-Warden, Debra Jones, Ineke Veerkamp and Ellen Scott (Rainbow Sistas Music/Sydney Spiritfest), Stephany Basia, Katherine Vavahea and Marcela Del Sol.

For your generous professional support with the creation of this book: Merle Conyer, Friederike Krishnabhakdi-Vasilakis, Jenni Nixon, Esther Olivares, Candy Royalle, Louise Wadley, Amalina Wallace and Wilfred C. Roach.

Special thanks to Georgina J.D. Abrahams, co-creator of Creative Womyn Down Under for fifteen years of enthusiastic support and especially for our wonderful children.

Finally, much love to Jai and Sofara for being a very encouraging captive audience during my performance poetry rehearsals and for providing thoughtful feedback on my work. You two are the pinnacle of all my blessings.

Freedom

Freedom Rap

performed with *djembe*

Freedom vibrates like the sound of my drum
Freedom vibrates like sound (*like sound*).

Journey MC on the mic.
May all of my words shed light
as all of my words take flight.

J to the **O** to the **U** to the **R** to the **N** to the **E**
to the **Y**'s a crooked letter, the more bent the better
I don't eat meat but I can rap hell for leather.
M-C stands for Mic Controller
When I'm on the microphone I might control
the words that flow, like lyrical percussion
a sonic expression, to make an impression
whatever my message I won't leave you guessing.

We all have a voice – make a choice to use it
shout out loud about life, and how you're living
proud of your decisions, have opinions
don't give in to anything that takes your freedom.

Freedom vibrates like the sound of my drum
Freedom vibrates like sound (*like sound*).

My drum represents my heartbeat
and since I'm alive then I have to be free
I'm going to live free from the shackles of society
that try to stifle me, that's my birthright you see.
But I don't take freedom for granted.
No I don't take freedom for granted.
Granted I've been granted many wishes that I'm grateful for
always had what I needed, and mostly more
but the *Freedom of Spirit* can't be bought
it takes love and self-respect
this can be hard fought, it takes *heart force*
just like the Freedom Fighters who have gone before
just like the Feminists who still battle for more.

You and I may not have a Nobel Peace prize
but when we honour ourselves
we can feel the noble peace rise.
That's how freedom begins
like a spark of love from deep within
Rising – Empowering – Inspiring.

So, what are we free to do?

End discrimination
all forms of abuse
and soul incarceration.
Erase racism, homophobia
and sexist connotations
religious segregations.

Vote against oppression
eliminate aggressive politics
impeach senseless politicians
sign marriage equality petitions.
Leave this precious world
and the animals we caretake
in a much better condition.

Make way for the musicians
poets and magicians.
Womyn with vision
in leadership positions.
People with a passion
for peaceful interactions.

Actively engage in conversations.
Gather information and
convey your observations.

The courageous are not allied with silence.
Poets are not allied with silence.

We participate, communicate
actively engaged in the world wide
campaign to transform hate
replacing ignorance with education;
we are the watchers
weaving words into action
we are the watchers
leaving words for revolution.

The courageous are not allied with silence.
That's why freedom vibrates
like the sound of my drum.
Freedom vibrates like sound.

Fire Belly Feminism

Academics, activists, poets and musicians
all advocating the same freedoms
to people in power who don't have to listen.

Feminism is it just another 'ism'
imprisoned by the paradigm of a time gone by?
Is it still alive?

I was born in the '70s; I was crawling on my knees
while women were marching in the street for liberty
so we all could be safe, we all could be free.

Not so long ago
I fell asleep in my own comfort zone.
The fire in my belly was out.
A flame was lit and brought to light
the plight of women's rights.
Our fight incessant against
violent aggression running rife.
We're still trying to reclaim the night.
…and the morning and the afternoon.

FREEDOM from fear, exploitation, violence
and abuse are international human rights.
Fire Belly Feminism is the fuel to ignite
our sisterhood reunite as we continue to break the silence.

This is an age-old war we are winning.
When we have won the world we know will disappear.
When we are done, it will mean the end
of centuries of terror, pain and fear.

Misogyny won't even be found in the dictionary.
Sexual assault, domestic violence and poverty
will be socially castrated
when women are truly liberated.
The strategy is not complicated.

We all need to safeguard the fire in our own belly.
Do whatever it takes to stay informed and awake.
Too many lives are at stake to let hearts freeze, eyes glaze.
Even when it feels too hard to stay engaged
we have an equal right to feel safe.

Throughout my life feminism
has not been able to take a break.
I hope that it can by the time
my five-year-old daughter is my age.

Weightless

I soaked my body in the ocean
and the waves carried my worries away with the tide.

I soaked my body in the ocean
and the water held me as I floated, weightless.

Thoughts washed through me, whispering at first:
Why don't all women feel weightless?
What's holding us down?

We long to be weightless.
We want to wait less time
to experience oppression on hiatus.

To be, to breathe – safe in our bodies
treated with equality, respected like queens.

Especially when women are expecting
There's no greater need than to avoid the debris
That prevents us from simply floating stress-free
Through the journey of a pregnancy.

However, strangers pat bellies
and share unwanted anecdotes
professionals are paid to test, prod and poke.

They weigh and measure babies
the same way they judge the mothers
and if they find us wanting
we must be willing to follow their advice
to smile and make nice or jeopardise a peaceful life
free from government intervention
once again, weightlessness is the price.

Women are not encouraged to listen to our intuition.
This is the beginning of the creeping questions
the self-doubt and guessing
even though the new life
that we carry is a blessing.

Medical model won't stop messing with our minds
projecting little mental missiles inside the messaging:

Mothers must rely on others
form institutional codependencies
and forget that we know best.
Forget that our maternal love is fearless.

Forget the TRUTH.
Just like the precious babies
in the oceans of our wombs
WE ARE WEIGHTLESS.

Humanitarian

Surely, humanity has evolved enough
to recognise the human rights being lost
neglected, even flaunted in front of us?

Of course, we're not told the whole story
we're only sold what will keep the masses distracted
but never long enough to become engaged, stay enraged.

Media commentaries comatose readers making us numb
leading us to believe nothing more can be done
than scrolling passively through volumes of information
on the latest flashing devices with tired thumbs.

Many of us have begun to lose control
heated words dangerously liquefied
erupting molten poetry from the mouth
firestarters for the volcanos in our hearts
dormant until now.

Yes. We have stopped holding our tongues
stopped holding onto comfortable indifference
stopped allowing the sanitisation of trauma
to ease our minds and misinform us.

We hold candlelight vigils and rituals
repurposing the internet to mobilise
prioritise and populate real-time events
where relief is physically felt and seen
as words are shared unscreened.

Horror truths so wretched
so clearly expressed
the audience needs to be
caught as they faint.
Caught. As. They. Faint.

Only in the compassionate spaces
can we begin to partially comprehend
humanitarian calls to tear down borders;
replace firearms with open arms
unbolt deadlocked doors on unscaleable walls
create accessible global citizenship
home, safety and freedom for all.

Equalities

Preaching
to the converted
will not hurt us.
It may help
to preserve us.
Even reimburse us
with trust lost
when justice
just is not
prevailing
found flailing
and sliding
through slip knots
dripping through
thin cracks
that aren't meant
to matter any more
but the syrupy evidence
of unconfessed atrocities
are smeared into
shiny marble floors
our nation's unspoken shame
swept under expensive carpets
along our parliamentary corridors.

Racism: Call it Out

Call it out. Call racism out.
Spoon-fed the solutions
Then it won't take forever
To create a revolution.

Put words in their mouths
Tools in their hands
Make them understand
It's an old battle but a new brand
Of weaponry: patience, perseverance
And a sturdy shield of empathy
Resilience, education, common decency
Vigilance, activism, bravery – call racism out.

The equation – discrimination over liberation
Reverse it and remove the temptation
To fall prey to a mindset of victimisation.

It's a very long day when you have to change ingrained beliefs
Even just believing something will change can bring relief
Thankfully it's not just up to me, individually
It takes a whole community to call it out – call racism out.

Racism can be subtle; excluding or wanting us to conform
From the planning of events to the filling out of forms
And the reinforcement of dominant social norms.

In our playgrounds, workplaces, out and about
Race discrimination doesn't always shout
So in every situation, make sure you call it out
It doesn't belong here – call racism out.

Spirituality Is In

Spirituality is in
The smell of the ocean
The hypnotic trance of the horizon out at sea
The gathering of storm clouds over a windy headland
The scent of rain on sun starched rocks before it even arrives.

Spirituality is in
Passionate conversations
And comfortable silences
Shared with friends.
Feeling connected to the people I love
Appreciating how blessed we are to journey together.

Spirituality is in
The holding of my babies
In those gentle seconds
As their weight shifts
And they fall asleep
Relaxed, in trusted arms.

Spirituality is in
A walk down to my local shops
Being present with every footstep
Noticing the breeze and the sunshine
And remembering what I wanted to buy.

Spirituality is in
Humour, joy, happiness and creativity.

Spirituality is in
'Greedy' time on my own
With a good-quality pen
And a blank piece of paper
Writing poetry.

Spirituality is in
The sound of a heartbeat drum song
Rippling around a fire circle of women
The pulse expanding in depth and resonance
As we all join in, playing as one.

Spirituality is in
The courage to live according to my values
Speaking my truth with loving kindness
Showing others the respect
And courtesy to do the same.

Spirituality is in
Resistance, activism, revolution and freedom.

Spirituality is in.
Spirituality is within.

Mind Journey

These days, I'm not much into writing rhymes
I'm spending time trying to climb
into the far reaches of my mind.
Designed to find 'enlightenment'
but am I meant to cling to that achievement?
Is that attachment?
Or true detachment?

My inward gazing eye
looks deep enough to see
the universal 'We'
one human family.
In fact, it seems to be one human factory
manufacturing all kinds of conclusions
like the 'separation' illusion fostering confusion
from individuals to Nation-state hate relations.
Why, when there are two 'I's in isolation
are we blind to the signs of unification?

Wars that divide
have a flipside
people also fight propaganda
when values collide.
The personal is global
so I search deep inside
until my heart reconnects with the vision quest
to journey – to travel, unravel mystical memories
subliminal tendencies to find my way home.
Consciously I reject the concept
that we are alone.
For we are all one.

Peace

Stop the battle. Relax.
Bring peace to the front of your mind.

Stop the battle. Unwind.
Break the broken record
Then forget it.
Don't push away
Or pull too close
Clutching plans
With empty hands.
Just drop into
This moment.

Stop the battle.
Experience the freedom
To stop looking, stop needing, stop wanting.
Stop grasping, regretting, not getting.

Stop the battle.
You are already
Breathing, being, living.
Believing in open eyes
Seeing emotions
And mind states as allies
Guiding you home
Into your deepest truth.

Stop the battle.
Relax. Unwind.
Experience the freedom
Of simply being.

Wise Woman

Edge of a forest
Winding leafy path
Shadows growing long
Soon it will be dark.

Gate in white picket fence
Beckons to a cottage
Aroma of baked bread
Fireplace lights windows.

'Wise woman' waiting within
Her mythical archetype
Holding space for the questions
Familiar only in dreams.

Creativity

Spoken Medicine

I only leave home for poetry.
Spoken medicine is my necessity.

The words we all breathe here
That we bleed here
Help us to remember
We are connected.

Spoken Word Psychiatrists
In this spotlight holding up a mirror
For the calculated seeping in of triggers
Resurrecting filtered reflections
On long forgotten feelings
Purified through the invocation
Of powerful lyrics.

Voices uncaged in a public forum
Leaking deepest secrets
To elicit inner peace
And integrate the hidden pieces
Of ourselves we all seek to meet with.

Slippery fragments of our soul
Lost within the psychological walls we build
Strong walls that we claw
When we cannot imagine a door any more.

Shell-shocked from the ceaseless
Horrifying noises of internalised war
That no one else ever hears
And even stitched-mouth silence ignores.

Until a venue is hired
Because someone inspired
Decided to organise.
A cover charge is paid
Stamp laid on the wrist and displayed
Like a medal of valour
Which will not be washed off for days
In hopes to keep the night close
As the insights and ink fades.

Every Poet to approach this mic centre stage
Is a Word Doctor, a Shaman, a Sage.
Administering spoken medicine.
Verbalising common experiences
Line after line injected into a hungry audience.

Wordsmith Physicians distilling life.
Prescribing the pharmaceutical benefits of poetry
Dispensed regularly to heal and build immunity
We deliver each verse surgically
And apply the welcoming balm
Of spoken word community.

I only leave home for poetry.
Spoken medicine is my necessity.

Creative Expression

Creativity is the courage
To put yourself into
Everything you do.

Being seen and vulnerable
Adding your own flavour
Colouring your environment
With your bravest choices.

Knowing who you are
Daring to reveal and share
Your unique, magnificent self.

Realigning your conscious intention
To be present, to show up
Ready to partake in magical artistry
Woven through daily experiences.

Noticing every opportunity
To act on your inspiration.
Honouring your sacred connection
With your life through creative expression.

The Problem With Poets

The problem with poets
Is that we feel everything.

We need to express
Every ripple of emotion
Passing through us.
Every single word
Needs a way to escape.

Pen and paper
A perfect valve
For the steam to release
And feelings to evaporate.

Emotions often prevent poets
From moving on with our day.
We delve into the human condition
Using creativity to document
The seeds of soul expression.

Words provide the power to explain
Feelings that will not be contained.
Without liberating our words
How would we remain sane?

The problem with poets
Is that we feel everything.

Everything.

Poetry What?

When I say 'Poetry' you say 'What?'
POETRY. (What?) Needs no invitation.
POETRY. (What?) Needs no permission.

So write and don't look back.
Never look back and be tempted
To hoard your words away
Inside a trophy cabinet, let them roam about
Motivating you to run after the most striking ones.

Run from the words
That reach out with barbed hands
Not satisfied simply to choke
Wanting to scar, permanently.

Run towards the kinder words
Like a checklist of love
In calligraphy on heart-shaped paper.

POETRY. (What?) Needs no invitation.
POETRY. (What?) Needs no permission.

Run a long-distance marathon
Waving your free verse at spectators as you pass by.
High-five the loyal ones who show up at every race
To celebrate 42.2 kilometres of your creativity.

Run yourself a bubble bath.
Relax as the louder conversations of the day fade
Allow your poetry (what?) to percolate.
Let new combinations of old words claim their space.

POETRY. (What?) Needs no invitation.
POETRY. (What?) Needs no permission.

Run head on as a way of being.
Use language to smash
The illusion of separateness.
Be the first one to smile at strangers.
Welcome them with well-crafted words
Spoken as if you were already friends.

POETRY. (What?) Needs no invitation.
POETRY. (What?) Needs no permission.

Run away with your poetry (what?)
Don't let the seduction
Of grammatically correct
Literary constructions
Restrict your flow.
Breathe your poetry (what?) like oxygen.

POETRY. (What?) Needs no invitation.
POETRY. (What?) Needs no permission.

So write and don't look back.
Never look back and be tempted
To hoard your words away.

Poetry Lab

Poets in the lab
Collaborators, narrators
Blowing the minds of rhyme-haters.
Times-changers, word-shifters
Activists with our pens and papers.

Gathering in cafes
Just like all the brave
Revolutionaries back in the day
Believing what we have to say
Can shape the world
Via verbal interventions
So, we bring our words
And our good intentions.

Soothsayers
Intuitive truth-players
Well-written
Nothing hidden
Present in the now
We have sound
Own the mic
Stand proud.

Poets. You've got this
And we've got your back.
We are creative community
At the Unpublished Poetry Lab.

A Poem Is Born

Present at the birth
Of my own poem.
Witnessing the experience
In surround sound.
A womb full of words
Bursts wide open
As if cascading
Over imagination's waterfall.

I am the midwife
Catching letters
As they float
Out into the world.
Wanting to be nurtured
Needing to be heard
Written down and held.

Newborn poetics
Conceived within
Spoken from heart
Airlifted from soul
To unpublished page.

Birthing Magic

Standing together on stage birthing a performance.
The magical places where friendship and creativity meet.
The same intimate feelings reserved only for lovers.
The harmonising bond between artists.
The passionate heart, soul and joy connection.
The pride born of perspiration and collaboration.
The dopamine rewards shared with appreciative audiences.
The personal fulfilment from this sacred partnership.

The vulnerability of co-creating performances with others
Is like relinquishing a significant piece of your identity
To be mixed inside a spinning test tube
Forming a new life over which you have no control.

You do not know if you will accept and nurture
Collaborated variations of your creative self.
So, you proceed with excited caution.

As though crafted by witches in the exchange of intuition
Every biological instinct spellbinds you to pro-create
To cross-pollinate and co-parent creativity
Until that enchanted moment when you are
Standing together on stage birthing a performance.

Written Word

I write. *I have to write.*
Thoughts bubble
sizzle and whistle
demanding attention
clouding up my head space
like a steaming kettle.

Words are colours
on a visual artist's palette.
I write on perfectly white
premium watercolour pages
designed for much more than
the scratchings of a ballpoint pen
painting heart symbols in English.

Words convincing evidence
that my fleeting feelings
captured on paper
are on some level real
and validate my existence.

I find a gentle peace within
believing I have been
heard, sustained and seen
by these once empty pages.

The words embrace me.
They witness and do not judge.
They offer a powerful mirror.
They provide a resolution.

Handwriting as bloodletting
to suspend spinning thoughts
spiralling in on themselves.

A wish, want or need
which repeats itself
and repeats itself
and in the process
gathers followers:
cling on thoughts.

Mounting an unstoppable campaign
of speedy, whizzing thinking
which cannot be ignored.

So, I write. *I have to write.*
to set my thoughts free
through written word.

Fifteen Reasons I Write

1   Witness my thoughts
2   Solidify into symbols
3   Conveying my life
4   Expression through syllables
5   ***Proving I exist.***

6   Reveal feeling emotions
7   Disrupt comfort zones
8   Honour truth found
9   Connecting us all
10   ***Proving we exist.***

11   Inspiration through vulnerability
12   Sculpting shared understanding
13   UNABLE TO STOP
14   Propelled by exchanging
15   ***Tokens of existence.***

Ballpoint Pen

It has to be a ballpoint pen
Solid.
Felt tips just don't feel like they can extract my feelings
The way I need them to be written.
Skating like silk across the page.
Somewhat distracted like a fair-weather friend
Only half listening, more concerned with how it looks.
Made for beauty rather than
The raw expressions of a life journey.

It has to be a ballpoint pen
Courageous.
Not afraid to form emotional words like hurt or rage.
Not gliding off into the next topic unfazed by content
Instead choosing to stay with me
Waiting, holding the place
Until through the ink
Difficult feelings begin to fade.

It has to be a ballpoint pen
Intuitive.
Rolling with the metaphoric punches.
Working with instinct and the vague hunches
That writers employ to relate a good story.
Loyal from the core of its twisting springs
There's no better friend than a ballpoint pen.

Artist Circles

Concentric rhythms
We dance our storylines.
We are five verses
Speaking of heart truths
In ageless sacred spaces.

Gathering of kinswomen
Holding the energy
Lighting the fire
Of creative expression.

Here we honour
Here we reclaim
Our creativity.

Shapeshifting
From doing to being.
Drummer to musician.
Poet to writer.
Songwriter to singer.

Thank you my Sisters.

Advice On What To Wear To a Poetry Reading

They will watch you closely
With their hearts and minds.
You may as well be standing
As naked as the words you speak.

Each syllable reborn.
Heard for the first time
In your particular order.

Every line is processed
Through the life-experience filters
Of unique individuals as they

Listen.
        Imagine.
                Visualise.

Like an actor in the wings
Swallow your stage fright
Inside a calm, deep breath
Dress up nervous energy with style.

Your clothes may not
Be noticed at all.
It's most important
How you choose to wear
The words you wrote
And have the courage to share.

Drumming Womyn

We drum life into dreaming
It's as vital as breathing.

Worlds we are weaving
Sister circles we sit in.

Every fibre of our beings
Alive inside these rhythms.

Untameable spirits of freedom
Connected forever within hearts drumming.

Drum Flow

I drum
And the drum
Plays me.

Reverberating
Peaceful feelings
Timeless unity
Musical spirituality

I drum
And the drum
Plays me.

Resonating
Heart beating
Journeying
Returning

I drum
And the drum
Plays me.

The flow
The pulse
The dance
The glow

I drum
And the drum
Plays me.

Djembe Dance

Wooden goblet, drink in the sounds
That bounce from the centre of the bass
To the edges of the tone and snap
One sip and there's no going back.

Djembe enchants the dancers
Fancy-hands on tribal rhythms
Enhances Tranceportation
Take the journey of imagination
To the heart of the drum beat's destination.

Listen with your heart. *Can you hear the call of the drum?*
Follow the bass. *That's right, follow the song of the bass.*

Flow with the rhythm. *Let the rhythm flow right through.*
Dance with the drum. *Can you feel the pulse of the drum?*

In your feet, on the earth – grounded in the joy of life.
In your feet, on the earth – free to be, yes free to be free.

With your hands in the air – let your body move everywhere
With your hands in the air – celebrate, yes celebrate.

Let the sound, let the dance – co-create, yes co-create.
Let the drum, let your heart – integrate, yes integrate.

Drum Song Sonnet

Chasing rhythms around the globe is fun.
From First Nations to Mother Africa
Celtic, Arabic and European
Polynesia to South America.

They play the same heartbeat on each bass drum
Merging universal soundscapes along
A journey of world groove continuum
Without words only powerful drum song.

Magic's made in the harmonisation
Djembes, bells, djuns, claves and shakarees.
There's an invisible fine vibration
Heard in circle when the music is played.

Strangers united through skins, rope and wood.
Everyone is equal and understood.

The Happen'n Drum Camp New York 2008

The Happen'n is *happening*.
Mesmerising energy of womyn drumming
Spirited sounds dancing out of the hall
Flying through the fire, skimming across the lake
Drums serenade each other
Communicating in smooth tones
Heartbeat drum at the pulse
24-hours in the zone, never alone
Like the voice of womyn
Which will not drown
In patriarchal oppression
The voice of womyn through percussion
Carries our survival celebrations
Drum circle communion
Creators of community
Strength, ritual and beauty
The voice of womyn in the rhythms
And in the silent spaces
In the pause for effect
Applause and respect
Of course we expect
Our intentions to womynfest
Anchored in moments like this
As monuments to the rich
Deep connections
Within ourselves
Sustained, honoured and upheld
By our Sistas with drums
We choose the Happen'n during busy lives
Because womyn have gathered this way
Since the beginning of time.

National Folk Festival 2008 – Folky Rap

Yo. We went to the F-O
Went to the F-O-L-K-Y.

The music is tight
Strings and wooden things
Voices harmonising
From angels without wings.

Spirit of sound
Inspiring souls
To take flight
Leave soaring
Wanting more
Looking forward
To the next fix
Of live music.

Injectable National Folk Festival
Invest in yourself
Expand your musical world
This right here is highly digestible
Recommendable.
Put your life on hold
It's suspendable.
Spend a long weekend
With International musicians
And Australian legends of dissent
All descended upon one space
Canberra, National Capital 'Meeting Place'.

National Folk Festival 2016 – Folky 50th

Nostalgic Aussie holiday smell of sun-warmed tent canvas; crisp tarpaulins and well-worn guide ropes lining dirt roads. Some shelters even poked into equestrian-quarters en route to the race track; the oval converted into a pop-up nomad city for the 50th National Folk Festival in Canberra.

Late night music rolls uphill out of the venues, blanketing the campgrounds with a welcome goodnight lullaby. Colliding rhythms rocking out at the edge of my senses as my body, tired and happy wrestles sleep from a magical day of heart-melting memories that social media photos can never accurately convey.

My two young children, their delighted faces captivated as Punch and Judy argued over who would mind the baby. Unrestrained laughter bursting out of wild wide smiles, surrounded by their peers, all with the innocent ability to be perfectly present chasing five days' worth of seasoned storytellers down rabbit holes with adventurous abandon in the same way we adults also allow ourselves to do during this most favourite long weekend.

My family and friends, we came here for the consciously curated creative community of musicians, poets, dancers, buskers, workshop givers, stallholders, food vendors, open mic and musical jam facilitators, crafts, arts and instrument makers, volunteers and the friendliest festy-goers on earth, half a century in the co-creating.

Each year I leave this festival of sound healing feeling blessed Yes. Deeply grateful to return home inspired and refreshed.

Dear Grace Cossington Smith

Sydney, 20 April 1892–20 December 1984

Dear Grace,

Thank you for conjuring spectacles of light
in unmixed vibrancy, illuminating canvas
with your rhythmical signature
of square broad strokes
pressed into the heart
of modernist art history
documenting Sydney
in bright thick layers
of animated paint
kaleidoscopes of
'Colour within colour'.

Thank you for your
spell-binding yellow interiors
that drew my breath
as they drew back your curtains
on a post-impressionist era
letting the world peer in
seeing life as you expressed it
through shining sunlit eyes.
Thank you for your vision and gifts
hanging in Australian galleries
much loved and prized.
Thank you for your
understated wisdom that
'Even the shadows are subdued light'.

Cossington Smith quotes courtesy of NSW Art Gallery.

Family

Jai

Standing at the precipice of parenthood
Waiting quietly at home
For the arrival of our firstborn
Peaceful in the calm of the unknown
Uncertainty surpassed by joy
Dreams of an enriched existence
Sharing life, expanding our families.

Nurtured by incredible support
Well wishes and best intentions
Sent with love and strength
From across the country
And around the world
To two starry-eyed mothers
Immersed happily in this
Rainbow village of loving kindness
Ready to raise a loving child.

Standing at the precipice of parenthood
We are not alone
We do not own
We will nourish body and soul
We will guide towards independence
We will provide generously
For his imminent journey of love and liberty
Jai!

Sofara

Precious baby daughter scooped up in my arms
I hold you close then swing you up, up, upwards
I enjoy your laughter at such fun.
Two lower teeth and four jutting through from above
In clear view as you smile at me with so much love.
I kiss your tiny feet resting in my palms
I've basked in 8 months of your sunshine
And summer has not yet begun.
Big eyes black against your golden skin
Search my face for comfort as you're coping with teething.
You try to bite my nose and chin
While inquisitive hands explore my eyes
Attempting to catch the sparkling.
I place you on the ground and watch you crawl about
Playing in your favourite spaces
Bongo drums, jumperoo, kitchen cupboards
Moving colourful magnets on the fridge.
Or racing down the hallway on your own
(With a cheeky grin flashed back to check I'm following)
To reach the container of toys in the bathroom
Which you examine and taste one by one
Then leave them gleefully thrown on the floor when done.
Crawling back to the lounge involves frequent stopping
To clap, dance and wriggle around
Always returning to the same play area
You find much better than any other
The empty chair at the kids' table
Right beside your beloved big brother.

Holidays

My two darling children asleep in the back seat
of 'Goldy' our old Ford Fairmont sedan
A miniature mobile home packed to bursting
with love, toys and essential treasures
on the way to Nanny and Poppy Jones 'holidays'.

New places to explore every day. Adventures.
Different beds to try out every night
along the east coast of Australia.
'Is this our new home, Mummy?'
Asks my four-year-old son Jai
wanting to make sense
of a carefree holiday life on the road.

'Where are we going today, Mummy?'
Planning where to go on the daily
Google-mapping how to get there.
Texting ahead to family and friends
dropping in for long overdue visits.

Spontaneous stops and charming surprises
like deserted ocean rock pools at low tide.
Water warming itself in the afternoon sun
laughing children, splashing and dancing
digging at the sand with red plastic spades
swirling heated salty sea ponds with outstretched hands
sitting side by side engrossed in aquatic discoveries
big brother and little sister with their whole lives ahead.
Sharing their precious early years in the cocoon
of a loving family with freedom to be themselves.

'I want to explore over here, Mummy.'
He runs towards a bigger rock pool
pointing his spade as if it were a telescope
successfully spying out new wonders.
I pick up my toddler as she struggles
through wet sand to follow him.
We all race along the beach together
and holler at the sunshine 'woo-hoo.'

They play ankle deep in sea water
scaring tiny fish which dart away.
She claps her hands and calls to me
delighted with her own cleverness
at tracking brother to the middle
of the shallow, sandy rock pool.

The joy and ease of family holidays
every moment gratefully celebrated
even when Sofara's runny nose attempts
to clog up her exuberance.
This little girl outshines any nuisance
with the strength of her spirit
learning from her big brother who likewise
brings so much more light to living.

Combined, my children dazzle me
with a fearless passion for exploring life.
I am their enthusiastic co-traveller
on this joyous parenthood holiday
of amazement, gratitude and grace.

Babies

Held gently
By their mothers
With deepest love.
Born into love.
Here because of love.

Two precious spirits
Shining out of newborn bodies.
Eyes awake to the beginning
Of a massive love-filled adventure.

Sensing love all around.
Listening to the voices of love
Recognised from the womb.

From their first twenty-four hours of life
Our babies knew they were
Wanted and tremendously loved.

The opportunity to raise
One child is a miracle.
Two loving children
Is twice as phenomenal.

Unbreakable

We are born
delicately fragile.
Breakable.

We need our parents love
Presence, capacity to care
Commitment, dedication
Whole-hearted devotion.

As we grow
They teach us by example
How to develop this great love
They have for us
Within ourselves.

Knowing we are deeply loved
Gives us lifelong resilience
In our ability to love
Courageously.

When we are raised
In an environment
Where love also radiates
From an entire community
Of family and friends;

We can become
Unbreakable.

I Used To Write

I used to write
of tiny hands
that closed inside of mine
perfect little gemstones.

I used to write
of cooing sounds
that drifted peacefully
from newborn smiley mouths.

I used to write
of the milestones
reached every single week
capturing miracles.

I used to write
compulsively on how
they 'complete me'
my darlings, my babies.

I used to write
daily right up until
they learned to crawl
then cruise about
wobble, shuffle, laugh, fall.

I used to write
volumes for them.
I hold those poems
close to my heart
so nothing is forgotten.

Ancestors

My children, our ancestors were not always free,
some of them born generations deep
into lifetimes of human slavery
stolen from the dreams they planned
with swollen, shackled feet and hands
to serve in plantation houses or work the land
breed more slaves, to live and die on command.

The bloodline of your grandmother's *whanau* (family)
seekers of peace treaties in the Pacific Ocean
who now share land they once owned.
Our queens dethroned but dynamically survived
to see her *tamariki* (children) thrive worldwide.

On your grandfather's side you are the descendants
of desert dwellers north of the African continent
his people from Egypt, Syria, Lebanon
war-torn countries traumatically rezoned
close relatives scattered and thrown
far from their homes by unrepentant regimes.

Cousins bearing arms against each other
who in much safer, luckier countries
would coexist peacefully as sisters and brothers.
Throughout history, geographical confines
have twisted and redefined our humanity
erasing at critical times the loving kindness
once connecting, once uniting our family ties.

Sweet Sherry

Grandmother's five o'clock sherry
gave her courage to face
each empty evening alone.

For three decades
since Grandfather passed
this ritual was done.

Enjoying her quarter glass
and sanctuary of memories
she had come to rely on
this gentle sunset meeting
with her sweet companion McWilliams.

Three children now grown and long gone
with children and grandchildren of their own.
So, at five o'clock every afternoon
my grandmother would sit alone.

Dinner almost ready in the oven
or simmering on the stove.
Reflecting on life's journey
goblet slowly turning in hand
as she gave silent prayers of gratitude
for her distant loved ones.

For my wonderful, greatly loved and missed Grandmother
Enid Clay (1910–1998)

Identity

Gabrielle

Name meaning 'God's bravest woman'

I am the daughter of Patricia Enid.
Granddaughter of Enid Ethel.
Great-granddaughter of Ethel Frances.

Nurture versus nature
versus the names
we choose to claim.

We can mistakenly chain
our destiny down to it.

We can change it when we
are no longer down with it
to rearrange the sound of it.

We grow up and some of us
are allowed to marry out of it.

We know intuitively that
we are not forever bound to it.

The meaning of our name
is what we make of it.

Personalities are not
powerlessly staked to it.

We can only hope our children
like their names and take to it.

If they break faith from it
fate has no complaint to make of it.

Personally, I tune into it
to the intention of my given name
Gabrielle 'God's bravest woman'.

When life manoeuvres me
to act with bravery
the courage I create
is strengthened
by my friends and family
invoking fearlessness
each time they
simply think of me
or speak my name.

* Name meaning from www.babynames.net

Adoption Belonging

I wear the hair and brown skin
of an unknown African-American.
I share the blood of Māori Ngāpuhi warriors.
Born on stolen Gadigal land, quite unfamiliar.

Adopted. Raised in a loving home.
White, educated, middle-class to the Left
where I like to keep my politics.

Biologically disconnected
my accent is not what is expected
I'm reminded in so many everyday ways
that my cultural heritage is public property
to be perpetually dissected.

There's nothing wrong
with asking someone where they are from.
Assuming they know, or were told
or were bold enough to splinter pretences
taking hold of their birthright to a genetic history
so their children and future generations
are not also held hostage by secrecy.

And so their responses to the innocent questions
of strangers at bus stops and in supermarket lines
are no longer shrouded in mystery.
The clouded irony of mix and match ancestry
providing all the answers that random people
seem urgently to need.

There is a natural curiosity
about kinship and family.
A tribal need to know
where we all belong;
where we are from.

As an adoptee
I can be reconnected
with my sense of identity
by remembering my own song.

Acknowledging the journey
I have travelled from
and knowing within
with an unshakeable faith
that I am right now
and have always been
exactly where I belong.

Journey MC

I'll just kick a little intro / let you know what's up with this afro on a Polynesian / I'm African-American / Māori Ngāpuhi / Australian geographically / born on Gadigal Country / always was and always will be.

Journey MC bringing rap back to my repertoire / sparking old school style / across synaptic gaps / in black hoodies and caps to cover grey matter / no matter / a middle-age rapper / those who mind don't matter / never mind the chitter chatter / whatever I'm down with the clever / words that make spoken medicine taste better.

And I never / forget to inject the rhythm / any topic given poetry's a prism / of enlightenment / not a prison / to serve time and hide within / it's a feast – yes a feast to be joining in all welcome to the table / where truth is five-star dining in / no harm in trying / that's why I am / home / on a microphone ready to rock it / lyrically / I drop, pop and lock it / like a soliloquy from my heart's pocket / I dance words into rhymes / write fascinating lines / ripe for the listening / change the world with poetry / leave eyes glistening.

This mic is an offering / so why don't we all begin / to say something? One thing? Anything? / Anything that conveys meaning / let us witness and birth into being / each other's dreaming / I feel like I'm preaching / when I scream please believe in / sharing your stories we need to be hearing / creating conversations / cracking open hearts and minds / unravelling and travelling / our collective storylines.

Flowetry

Change takes time / so take your time / be in the flow / be in your flow / be the flow / flowetry.

Spinning on my heels waiting for change / that's not going to come / if I'm not changing my ways / if I'm enabling inaction to determine my fate / forget letting others have a free reign life rots in a haze / people pleasing as my soul is willingly given away / it's no place to stay / no safety in place replacing fear with self-love / I'm bringing courage and grace / so get out of my way / get out of my way / I'm breaking old habits watch me throw them away / a day at a time / is all that it takes / by my side / my family and my great mates.

I'm the narrator, creator of my present day / I'm the change-maker / the destiny-raker / the orchestrator of happiness / it's my bliss and my wager / I bet on myself all the way to make it.

I've undertaken to become the uncager / of unnecessary misery / setting free negativity / I'm discerning burning bridges with my intuition / using all six senses to eradicate suspicions of narcissism / scrutinising those invited into my life / I don't always get it right / but change takes time / yes change takes time / so take your time / be in the flow / be in your flow / be the flow / flowetry.

Simply Me

It's not complicated / so don't complicate this / you see with me its simple / you get what you see / you get what you see / do you get what I mean? / With me its simple / you get what you see / take me as you find me I'm Journey MC.

Yes I'm on a journey / returning / to how I used to be / I used to see / the best in everybody / till life tested me wildly / but I survived and I still try to treat people kindly / keep the past behind me / I used to trust blindly / like a fool who wouldn't agree / that hearts can break and bleed / I let the Universe lead / believed that life was out to get me / everything I'd ever need / no need for greed / no need to wear a mask or ask friends for ID / you see with me its simple / you get what you see / you get what you see / do you get what I mean? / With me its simple / you get what you see / take me as you find me I'm Journey MC.

From early on I was gone / in love with life for the invite born on a Friday 13 / because I'm lucky / my glass is half-full because it's never been empty / raised in this land of plenty / gifted this brief existence / a single second / in eternity so everyday I choose to / BE present / BE the flow / STAY connected /BE Journey MC / Master of Clarity / I like to be clear / it's taken me 44 years / to be myself / see myself rarely told / I deserved to be heard / I've learnt my worth / earnt my birthright to MY life / my life as I please / so please take it from me / take me as you find me or leave / You see with me its simple / you get what you see / take me as you find me I'm Journey MC / It's not complicated / so don't complicate this.

Forty-four

Forty-four years
I've learned the wisdom of 'freedom'
Building resilience through heart lessons.

Forty-four years
I've found the birthplace of 'creativity'
Is in the out-breath of every living thing.

Forty-four years
I've discovered that 'family' of choice
Is the lifeblood of happiness and secret of joy.

Forty-four years
I've defeated fierce forces for my 'identity'
Unable to keep me in boxes without keys to the locks.

 Gabrielle Journey Jones was born on Gadigal land, Sydney, and is from Māori and African-American blood-lines. Adopted into a loving family, she grew up in Canberra.

Gabrielle has performed her poetry at local, national and international events in diverse venues including Sydney Opera House, Friend in Hand Glebe, Kent Street Café, Radio Skidrow, Django Bar, Women's Library, 'Woman Scream' Festival NSW Parliament House, Sydney Summer Spiritfest, 'Rebellious Words' Red Rattler 2016 and Pride Carnival Alice Springs. She is the winner of open mic and slam events including Word Salad 2017 launch; 'Say It Sing It' South Coast Writers Centre and Enough Said Poetry Slam Wollongong 2016; 'Bad Slam No Biscuit Poetry Slam' Canberra National Folk Festival 2016; and Caravan Slam Marrickville 2015. She was a finalist in the Australian Poetry Slam Sydney Slam 2016.

Gabrielle has been involved with many not-for-profit community organisations and government agencies across Australia during her twenty-year career as a social worker. Gabrielle is co-founder and CEO (Creativity Encouragement Officer) of Creative Womyn Down Under, a community initiative established in Sydney, 2006 to connect women and many forms of creative expression. Gabrielle combines creativity and social work ideals in her poetry workshops and drum circles.

The launch of *Spoken Medicine* in 2017 with Ginninderra Press completes a year of dynamic poetry community collaborations. Gabrielle joined the Red Room Company to deliver poetry workshops in schools in NSW. Red Room is committed to making poetry a meaningful part of everyday life. Gabrielle also became a member of the South Coast Writers Centre board of management. Gabrielle contributed to the inaugural Unspoken Words festival this year and will join the team of artistic directors in 2018.

Creativity as social, political and personal action is the cornerstone of Gabrielle's work as a performance poet. The words in this collection are best enjoyed read out loud.

Contact Gabrielle via www.creativewomyn.net

www.ingramcontent.com/pod-product-compliance
Lightning Source LLC
Chambersburg PA
CBHW062149100526
44589CB00014B/1761